PAUL
HARVEY'S
FOR WHAT
IT'S WORTH

Bantam Books by Paul Harvey, Jr.

Paul Harvey's The Rest Of The Story
More Of Paul Harvey's The Rest Of The Story
Destiny and 102 Other Real-Life Mysteries

Bantam Books Edited by Paul Harvey, Jr.
Paul Harvey's For What It's Worth

PAUL HARVEY'S

FOR WHAT IT'S WORTH

Edited by Paul Harvey, Jr.

Compiled by Liz Murray
Art Direction by Paul Harvey, Jr.
and Liz Murray
Illustrations by Scott Harris

BANTAM BOOKS
NEW YORK · TORONTO · LONDON · SYDNEY · AUCKLAND

PAUL HARVEY'S FOR WHAT IT'S WORTH
A Bantam Book / June 1991

Library of Congress Cataloging-in-Publication Data:

Harvey, Paul, 1918–
[For what it's worth]
Paul Harvey's for what it's worth / edited by Paul Harvey, Jr. ;
compiled by Liz Murray ; art direction by Paul Harvey, Jr., and
Liz Murray.
p.   cm.
ISBN 0-553-07720-1
1. American wit and humor.   I. Harvey, Paul.   II. Title.
PN6162.H3574   1991
081—dc20   91-8083
                                                          CIP

Published simultaneously in the United States and Canada

PRINTED IN THE UNITED STATES OF AMERICA

RRH   0 9 8 7 6 5 4 3 2

Hello, Americans:

You wrote this book.

Axiomatically, noise makes news. Page one is usually preoccupied with wrongdoers and wrong-doing, with malfeasance, misfeasance, mistakes and tragedies. With the one in a million planes which does not land safely.

So over the years I have sought to make the hard, cold facts a bit more palatable.

You, from Main Street, USA, have advised me of humorous hometown experiences which otherwise I might never have known about.

On each broadcast I have included at least one such item under the heading: "For What It's Worth."

For several years family, friends and listeners have asked for a written copy of some of these "truth-is-funnier-than-fiction" stories.

So here they are.

You wrote this book.

Thank you.

Paul Harvey

EDITOR'S NOTE

The cheerful little anthology you are about to read —and will much enjoy—is more than intrinsically enjoyable. I believe it is a journalistic treasure.

For years newscasters have sought to sprinkle a bit of sugar along with the salt and pepper. It was Paul Harvey who taught them to, but no one has ever been able to teach them how.

The Paul Harvey style is inimitable—a fact due partly to his selection of news stories and partly to his treatment of them. Nowhere among the many journalistic nuances invented by Paul Harvey is that more evident than in his selection and treatment of that last news item in each broadcast, which his twenty-two million loyal radio listeners happily anticipate as the **"For What It's Worth Department."**

If the selection process is, in Paul Harvey's own simile, like "panning for gold," I have particularly admired, as editor for this collection, the author's secondary role as the craftsman "jeweler." And so I have left each printed page of this wonderful document as it appeared in the broadcast of the date subscribed, with the punctuation and dynamics almost precisely as originally infused.

I feel you will, as I did, hear the voice of the author emerging from the manuscript.

Happy Reading!

Paul Harvey, Jr.

Our **For What It's Worth Department** hears from Hershey, Pennsylvania—where the woman in the Mercedes had been waiting patiently for a parking place to open up.

The shopping mall was crowded.

The woman in the Mercedes zigzagged between rows—then up ahead she saw a man with a load of packages head for his car.

She drove up and parked behind him and waited while he opened his trunk and loaded it with packages.

Finally he got in his car and backed out of the stall.

But before the woman in the Mercedes could drive into the parking space . . .

A young man in a shiny new Corvette zipped past and around her and HE pulled into the empty space and got out and started walking away.

"Hey!" shouted the woman in the Mercedes, "I've been waiting for that parking place!"

The college-ager responded, "Sorry, lady; that's how it is when you're young and quick."

At that instant she put her Mercedes in gear, floorboarded it, and crashed into and crushed the right rear fender and corner panel of the flashy new Corvette.

Now the young man is jumping up and down shouting, "You can't do that!"

The lady in the Mercedes said, "That's how it is when you're old and rich!"

May 22, 1987

Our **For What It's Worth Department** knows why the firemen want new helmets in Fairfax County, Virginia . . .

The helmets they have now are colorful, high-impact plastic, adjustable to size and resistant to scuffing . . .

Just one thing:

Near heat, they melt.

October 26, 1977

For What It's Worth . . .

Ed Ruffing reports in the Utica, New York, *Observer-Dispatch.*

Burglars in suburban Marcy were carrying the TV set from the house down the driveway when the next-door neighbor called out:

"Hey, are you going to fix her television set?"

And the burglars called back, "Yes."

And the neighbor asked, "Mine needs fixing, could you take it, too?"

And the burglars said, "Be glad to."

And they did.

November 9, 1978

Our **For What It's Worth Department** has decided . . .

In the wake of Chicago's worst-ever winter . . .

NOW it can be told:

When all of our rooftops were loaded, many overloaded with snow . . .

Robert McGrath saw his wife go into the backyard garage to fetch some boxes.

Seconds later he heard the crash.

Looking out he saw the roof of the garage had caved in.

McGrath did not stop for hat or coat . . .

He ran from the house—grabbed a snow shovel—and called out for neighbors to help.

Yelling and digging and his sweat freezing on his face—throwing snow and pulling away boards—he heard her voice—then saw her hand!

He kept digging and throwing and pulling . . .

And within minutes he had his wife in his arms and was sobbing, "Are you all right? Are you all right?"

She was all right.

I would not tell what I am about to tell except that a neighbor saw and snitched . . .

Mrs. McGrath—had gone into the garage through one door and out through another.

She was safe in the house when she looked out and saw her husband digging and shouting orders and throwing lumber and she could not let her gallant rescuer down.

She put her coat on again and went back out and went back in through the back door of the garage—and allowed husband Bob to be her hero.

March 29, 1979

Danny Layne, reporting from Jacksonville, North Carolina, tells our **For What It's Worth Department . . .**

A Chrysler dealer is urging car buyers to "buy American".

Calls his promotion BE AMERICAN, BUY AMERICAN.

And purchasers of a new AMERICAN car get a free chance on a Japanese motorcycle.

January 3, 1981

6

Our **For What It's Worth Department** understands . . .

At the South Central Bell office, Jackson, Mississippi . . .

A secretary returned from her coffee break to see her boss, Jim McGowan, sitting at *her* desk.

HE SAID:

"Sorry, I had a headache and took the liberty of looking in your desk for some aspirin." Said he'd taken two and felt "better now".

SHE SAID:

"Anytime, Mr. McGowan."

"And," she added, "you won't get pregnant, either."

September 29, 1983

Our **For What It's Worth Department** hears from Pretoria, South Africa . . .

Where a newspaper has been trying to correct a classified ad.

Because the ad, as it was first printed, said, quote:

The Rev. A. J. Jones has color TV set for sale. Telephone 555-1313 after 7 P.M. and ask for Mrs. Donnelley who lives with him, cheap.

So . . . the next day the Pretoria paper printed a correction, quote:

We regret any embarrassment caused to Rev. Jones by a typographical error in yesterday's editions. It should have read, "The Rev. A. J. Jones has color TV set for sale, cheap. Telephone 555-1313 and ask for Mrs. Donnelley who lives with him after 7 P.M."

Then the *next* day . . . the paper said:

The Rev. A. J. Jones informs us he has received several annoying telephone calls because of an incorrect advertisement in yesterday's paper. It should have read, "The Rev. A. J. Jones has color TV set for sale. Cheap. Telephone after 7 P.M. 555-1313 and ask for Mrs. Donnelley who loves with him."

ONE DAY LATER . . .

Please take notice that I, the Rev. Jones, have no TV set for sale. I have smashed it. I have not been carrying on with Mrs. Donnelley. She was until yesterday my housekeeper.

Yesterday one more ad:

WANTED a housekeeper. Telephone the Rev. A. J. Jones 555-1313. Usual housekeeping duties, good pay, love in.

End quote.

November 8, 1978

Our **For What It's Worth Department** has been talking to Harry Bane of Lake Oswego, Oregon . . .

Says he has quit jogging . . .

Says he accepted our suggestion that jogging is good for you . . .

And he tried it . . .

But he has quit.

Says the wind keeps putting out his cigarette.

December 12, 1977

D_{r.} Martin MacIntyre is sharing with our **For What It's Worth Department** something very personal today . . .

A note from his small daughter.

Yesterday the Potomac, Maryland, dentist refused to allow his daughter Sarah to go to the pool for the third time in one day . . .

He just said no and that was that.

So—last evening—Sarah, age six, wrote a note in red pencil and left it on her daddy's pillow.

It said:

Daddy—I hate you.

And it's signed, *Love—Sarah.*

September 13, 1977

For What It's Worth . . .

Jackson Jimmy Ward remembers a lower California earthquake . . .

As it hit, an anxious grandmother ran to the back door screaming, "Johnny!"

And the youngster responded, "*I* didn't *do it,* Grandma."

January 12, 1981

Our **For What It's Worth Department** can't decide whether this is a bargain.

I have right here in front of me—an ad under FOR SALE in the Marshfield, Wisconsin, newspaper:

FOR SALE. PARACHUTE. ONCE USED. NEVER OPENED. 555-9923.

August 7, 1981

Our **For What It's Worth Department** reads the San Diego *Union* survey of high school students.

The survey asked:

"Do you approve advertising condoms on television?"

66% of the students polled replied that they favored the idea.

26% were opposed to advertising condoms on TV.

8% replied that regardless of the ads, President Reagan should continue to send them military aid.

September 23, 1987

Our **For What It's Worth Department** has set this aside long enough now . . .

About what happened to Bryan Wolfe of Sugar Grove, Oregon.

Bryan drove out into the countryside—down a dirt road beyond Beaver Pond—to a safe place to do some target shooting.

He plinked away at some tin cans which he'd parked on the stump of a hollow tree.

Hollow tree stump sawed off about five feet high.

One of his targets fell down into the hollow of the tree.

Bryan leaned down . . .

Reached into the pit . . .

A little farther . . .

And suddenly he slipped.

I mean he slipped head first down *into* the hollow tree.

He's out there all alone—miles from anywhere—and he's stuck upside down in a hollow tree!

No way he could back up and out, and no way anybody could hear him holler.

It was six and a half hours before a state forestry crew happened by that way—saw his parked car and then saw two boots sticking up out of an old hollow tree stump.

Carefully they pulled his swollen body from the hole.

That was enough days ago so the swelling's gone down.

The cuts and bruises are only a little apparent.

But now he has to go back to work and listen to all those smart aleck remarks.

November 20, 1990

Our **For What It's Worth Department** believes this has to be the quote of the week.

Actor James Garner—from his hospital bed—telling how it happened, said:

"The guy ran up to my car, grabbed me through the window and began to beat me. I fell out the car door onto the ground and the man kicked me—repeatedly.

"But I could tell he was tiring.

"If he'd kept it up for five more minutes, I'd have had him."

End quote.

January 18, 1980

Our **For What It's Worth Department** hears from St. Paul United Church of Christ in Columbus, Ohio . . .

Music director Dennis Avey—visiting elementary Sunday School—overheard an eight-year-old leading the class in prayer.

And he wrote it down.

The lad said, "God bless our mothers and our fathers and our teachers and our brothers and our sisters—and please take care of Yourself, God; if anything happens to You, we're sunk!"

February 16, 1981

F**or What It's Worth** . . .
   In the Riviera Trattoria restaurant . . .
   Lake Street in Kirkland, Washington . . .
   I think the sign means NO SMOKING.
   What it says is:
   IF WE SEE YOU SMOKING WE WILL ASSUME YOU ARE ON
FIRE AND TAKE APPROPRIATE ACTION.

January 18, 1989

21

Our **For What It's Worth Department** understands . . .

The TV program *Laverne and Shirley*—is shown in
Bangkok, Thailand—where women do not act like
that.

So each program is preceded with a subtitle which
says, quote:

"The two women depicted in the following epi-
sode are from an insane asylum. . . ."

July 9, 1979

22

Our **For What It's Worth Department** has learned about the sculpture in San Jose, California . . .

One of those twenty-foot metal sculptures . . .

Authorized by the City Council . . .

Called "Great Planes [sic] Study Number Seven" . . .

It's been destroyed by workmen with bulldozers. They thought it was junk.

Worse, they smashed and removed the metal sculpture more than a year ago and somebody just now noticed it's missing.

Worse . . .

City officials will pay the artist twenty-five thousand dollars to replace it.

October 20, 1986

Our **For What It's Worth Department** knows why *Cappers* does not name the airline . . .

But passengers say the takeoff was already delayed when the pilot came on the intercom to announce:

"There's a warning light for the thermal expander valve on the number two engine and I will not fly until it is replaced. Please return to the terminal waiting room."

The passengers were off the plane only ten minutes when they were told to get aboard again.

The passenger from Hartland, Minnesota, asked a flight attendant, "Did they get the new thermal expander valve already?"

And the attendant said, "My land, no! There's not one of those things within a thousand miles. They got us a new pilot."

July 4, 1989

25

Our **For What It's Worth Department** hears from Anaheim, California—where a bank robber strode into a bank yesterday and demanded money.

But it was a bankrupt bank.

Hasn't had any money for two months.

The only people in the place were government officials . . .

FDIC auditors trying to figure out where the bank's money went.

The would-be bank robber got away.

Because the officials in the bank didn't report the caper for two hours.

Took them that long to stop laughing.

May 9, 1984

Manager Tommy Lasorda of the Los Angeles Dodgers has confessed to our **For What It's Worth Department;** he told on himself what I am about to tell you.

On the road in Cincinnati . . .

Went to Sunday morning mass . . .

And whom should he see just across the aisle but his rival manager, John McNamara of the Reds.

Their two teams were to play later that day.

They eyed each other but neither spoke.

When the service was over, McNamara knelt to pray—then, on his way out, lit a votive candle.

Lasorda—on his way out—blew it out.

June 4, 1982

27

Our **For What It's Worth Department** is told that Allen Michael is running for President.

Allen Michael, 66, of Stockton, California, might be the man you're looking for.

He has ALL the answers—to inflation, unemployment, environment, health care and war.

Mr. Michael says he got the answers . . .

When he was beamed aboard a flying saucer in 1947.

April 5, 1983

For What It's Worth . . .

Divorce in Pôrto Alegre, Brazil.
Brazilian farmer Romeo Bitencourt . . .
Is 90.
Married 65 years.
12 children, 50 grandchildren, 36 great-grandchildren.
Divorced. He says . . .
"Incompatibility".

April 2, 1979

Our **For What It's Worth Department** wants you to know what Carl Coleman told *Quote* magazine.

He was driving to work when a woman motorist, passing too close, snagged his fender with hers.

Both cars stopped.

The young woman surveying the damage was in tears.

It was her fault, she admitted.

But it was a new car—less than two days from the showroom.

How was she ever going to face her husband?

Mr. Coleman was sympathetic but explained they must note each other's license number and automobile registration.

She reached into the glove compartment to retrieve the documents in an envelope . . .

And on the first paper to tumble out, in a heavy masculine scrawl, were these words:

"In case of accident, remember, Honey, it's you I love, not the car."

April 16, 1984

Our **For What It's Worth Department** understands that Police Chief Clifton Sullivan—Russell Springs, Kentucky—got a call from a lady who wanted her bachelor neighbor arrested for indecent exposure.

The Chief went to her house and witnessed for himself . . .

The fact that the man next door was in his bathroom shaving.

But, the Chief said, "With the bottom part of the man's bathroom window covered as it is, I cannot tell whether the bottom part of the man is wearing anything or not."

But, the woman said, "Well . . . you just stand on this chair and stand on your tiptoes and you'll see!"

December 6, 1978

Does our **For What It's Worth Department** have time to add this?

Sports Illustrated reports from Dade County, Florida . . .

Ronald Bradley, 21, goes to prison for three years for burglary.

On several break-ins he carefully wore gloves.

But . . .

He wore GOLF GLOVES—the kind that left his fingertips naked.

June 20, 1978

Our **For What It's Worth Department** . . .

Reads the Wisconsin-Bell employee newspaper. Under FOR SALE:

Wedding dress with train and chapel length veil, size nine, never worn, $250.

The same ad also offers: *Smith & Wesson pistol.*

Used once?

September 2, 1985

35

Our **For What It's Worth Department** hears from Syracuse, New York—where a woman went to the hospital with a cockroach in her ear.

Doctors Warren and Rotello promptly shot a squirt of lidocaine into her ear.

That is supposed to cause the critter to exit the ear on its own.

But the cockroach stayed put.

They sprayed a DOUBLE dose of lidocaine into her ear.

The woman is screaming but the bug is not budging.

That is when the doctors reached for a suction device on the wall—a suction device used to suck up excess liquid spills—and they inserted the tip of the suction device into the woman's ear—and the suction device sucked the cockroach—"shloop"—onto the tip and the tip and the roach were withdrawn pronto.

Doctors Warren and Rotello are not taking credit for this ingenious retrieval method.

They say it was the woman's idea.

It was she who gave them the idea when she shouted, "Get that sucker out of there!"

February 2, 1989

37

Our **For What It's Worth Department** predicts that the United Presbyterian Church in Spencerport, New York, will be packed.

This week's church bulletin promises that "both church choirs will sin together."

More? All right.

From the South Minneapolis Church Newsletter, quote: *Tomorrow afternoon there will be meetings in the north and south ends of the church. Children will be baptized at both ends.*

End quote.

February 17, 1978

Our **For What It's Worth Department** is aware that the community of Speedway is an Indianapolis suburb.

SPEEDWAY is where the Indianapolis SPEED-WAY is located.

It was in SPEEDWAY that police stopped and arrested a motorist for drunk driving.

They took the accused drunk driver to the police station—allowed him to make his one telephone call.

Which he did.

Within minutes all phones were ringing off the wall—there and everywhere. Townspeople calling to complain they had no water—their water had been cut off!

Eventually the police remembered the guy they'd arrested for drunk driving—was named Max Williams.

And they remembered he'd made a phone call.

And they remembered that Max Williams is Supervisor of the City Water Department!

January 21, 1982

Our **For What It's Worth Department** visits Altoona, Pennsylvania . . .

Where TV anchorman Brandon Brooks demonstrated for his viewers how to protect their homes from burglars.

He used his own home to demonstrate . . .

Double locks on doors, windows that will not open from the outside, burglar alarms . . .

Now it appears that thieves were watching the program.

They not only learned where the double locks were, but where the TV set was and the VCR and the furniture and other things.

So nights later—while Brandon Brooks was on the air back at the studio—the thieves broke into his house and cleaned him out.

That window that won't open from the outside: they smashed it.

March 6, 1987

Shirley Luke—Sylvester, Georgia—tells our **For What It's Worth Department** that she went into the beauty shop—and asked that her hair be cut "like Geraldine Ferraro's".

The beauty operator said . . .

She swears the beautician said . . .

"You'll have to describe it; I don't watch the soap operas."

October 22, 1984

Our **For What It's Worth Department** concedes . . .

That spying against our government is being discouraged—not by patriotism—but by "bugs".

In a courtroom in Los Angeles an accused American spy and his Soviet girlfriend are having to listen to recordings of themselves lovemaking in the backseat of a car.

Even edited, the dialogue is embarrassing:

"I'll eat you for my dessert; you are so sweet."

"Go home before I attack you (again)."

There are giggles and other words.

Sounds of kissing and . . . other words. Then these significant ones . . .

His voice: "You have stolen my heart."

Her voice: "I know . . . it's my job."

August 22, 1985

The Kilgore, Texas, *News-Herald* reports to our **For What It's Worth Department** . . .

Motorist removed unconscious from his wrecked car and carried to a nearby gas station.

Then he came to.

Opened his eyes and began to struggle violently.

Eventually he was subdued and removed to a hospital.

Asked later why he had struggled to get away from his rescuers—he explained.

They'd taken him to a SHELL station.

And somebody was standing in front of the "S".

March 15, 1979

Our **For What It's Worth Department** reads in the Sioux City *Journal* under LOST AND FOUND.

Quote:

Wandered in—largest German shepherd I have ever seen.
Young male.
Please come get him.
Call 555-4742 after six.
P.S. Retrieves concrete blocks.

June 21, 1983

Our **For What It's Worth Department** overhears an exchange of words—on an airliner between Chicago and Las Vegas.

Muhammad Ali was a passenger.

Confronted by a flight attendant who said he would have to fasten his seat belt . . .

Muhammad Ali replied, "Superman don't need no seat belt."

To which she, the flight attendant, replied—sweetly—"Superman don't need no airplane."

June 20, 1980

Our **For What It's Worth Department** understands . . .

That in Sydney, Australia, a woman was thrown from her horse.

Miss May Southgate was riding horseback when —she says—a helicopter swooped down so low that it spooked her horse and she was thrown off.

And she sued.

The helicopter crew insisted that if Miss Southgate had been wearing proper riding boots she'd not have fallen off.

The court deduced that riding boots had little to do with it—that the helicopter crew swooped down so low because of something else she was not wearing.

She was wearing only half of a two-piece swimsuit.

March 27, 1987

Our **For What It's Worth Department** knows you've heard lawyers on TV advertising themselves . . .

Rob Moore in the Orlando, Florida, *Sentinel* . . .

Caught one such ad on his tape machine.

The spokesperson lawyer at the beginning of the TV ad says, quote:

"If you or any member of your family has been killed . . ."

August 8, 1986

Our **For What It's Worth Department** is aware as you are that Charles Forte is London's most renowned hotel man—distinguished—instantly recognizable by one and all.

A young man lunching at the Strand . . .

Left his table . . .

Quickly sought out Mr. Forte . . .

Asked for a favor.

The young diner said he wanted to impress his table companions . . .

So would the esteemed hotelier—Mr. Forte—drop by his table just to greet him.

A short while later, Charles Forte obliged—stepped up to the young man's table—greeted him—and the young man said: "Forte—don't bother me now. Can't you see I'm busy!"

February 9, 1987

Our **For What It's Worth Department** has learned that at William and Mary College in Virginia there is a faculty member—Dr. Mitchell Byrd—and Dr. Byrd teaches a course about birds.

Sometimes he goes up in a light plane or helicopter—to count eagles and ospreys in their nests.

That explains yesterday.

The telephone caller to William and Mary asked to speak to an ornithologist.

The caller was told, "That would be Dr. Byrd."

"You have an ornithologist named Byrd?"

"Yes. But he's not here right now; he's out flying."

"You have an ornithologist named Byrd and he's out flying?"

"That's right. Would you care to leave a message?"

"I don't think so."

February 3, 1987

Lori Pavich, reporting to our **For What It's Worth Department** . . .

Sees a sign in a parking lot in Livermore, California.

Sign says, PARKING RESERVED FOR CLIENTS OF DEL VALLE PET HOSPITAL. VIOLATORS WILL BE NEUTERED.

April 18, 1989

Our **For What It's Worth Department** hears that Ann Connolly was in the Red Food Store in Knoxville, Tennessee—shopping for groceries.

While she was momentarily distracted somebody snatched her purse from her shopping cart.

Now, Miss Connolly is a real estate broker . . .

Carries one of those talk-back beeper devices for telephone paging . . .

Carries it in her purse.

She hurried to the manager's office telephone and dialed herself. Then spoke into the phone *knowing* her voice would be transmitted through the beeper in her missing purse.

Because she always carried the beeper in her purse she had the beeper turned up good and loud.

Produce manager says you should have seen that surprised man standing there with her purse . . .

And the purse was talking . . .

And the voice was saying . . .

"Take this purse to the manager's office immediately."

And he did!

June 7, 1985

Our **For What It's Worth Department** eavesdrops on a meeting of the Wayne Central Board of Education . . .

With 1976 behind them, the assembled heard a report from Assistant Superintendent of Schools Gerald Greenstein.

And he presented to the Board a collection of excuses which parents had written to teachers this past year.

One says: *My son is under doctor's care and should not stay in school this afternoon; please execute him.*

One says: *Please excuse Blanche from physical education for a few days. She fell from a tree and misplaced her hip.*

Here's Superintendent Greenstein's favorite—

Dear school: Pleas exkuse John from being absent October 28, 29, 30, 31, 32, 33.

It's signed, *Cincerely.*

Spelled with two "C"s.

January 11, 1977

Our **For What It's Worth Department** acknowledges it's April 16!

The Internal Revenue Service office in Jacksonville, Florida, has heard from a woman who says she was *not in the mood* to file an income tax return yesterday; she promises to file two returns next year.

She was advised to get in the mood now.

One taxpayer sent a letter asking, *Please remove my name from your mailing list.*

Nice try.

In tax court in New York City, Judge Howard Dawson is prepared for any argument . . .

One taxpayer claimed, "As God is my judge I do not owe this tax."

Judge Dawson replied, "He isn't. I am. You do. Next case."

April 16, 1987

Our **For What It's Worth Department** understands that actor Robert Redford is in Santa Fe, New Mexico, making a movie . . .

In and around town between takes . . .

But the lady who encountered him in an ice-cream parlor on Canyon Street was determined to stay cool . . .

She pretended to ignore the presence of the movie star . . .

But after leaving the shop she realized that she did not have the ice-cream cone she'd bought and paid for.

She returned to the shop . . .

To ask for her ice-cream cone.

Overhearing, Robert Redford said, "Madame, you'll probably find it where you put it—in your purse."

September 10, 1986

For What It's Worth . . .

Midwest Burger King was robbed last night.

Police have arrested . . .

Are you ready for this?

Burger King was robbed last night and police have arrested eighteen-year-old Ronald McDonald.

April 5, 1979

Our **For What It's Worth Department** reads from the Dover, Ohio, newspaper. I quote:

Husband says either he or puppies must go. Puppies are playful and cute. Husband is grouchy and unsympathetic. Your choice free.

Signed *Mrs.* Jim Cook.

February 2, 1981

World evangelist John Haggai tells our **For What It's Worth Department** about the civic dinner in London . . .

Where a woman guest was seated alongside a visitor from *China.*

The Chinese remained silent—until finally the lady asked: "Likee soupee?"

And the Chinese nodded, said nothing.

The conversation lapsed.

After coffee was served the speaker of the day was introduced and it turned out to be the visiting Chinese.

He talked for twenty-five minutes in impeccable English—about the sociological significance of the European Common Market.

And amid applause, returned to his seat.

And turned to the lady seated next to him and asked: "Likee speechee?"

January 4, 1978

Our **For What It's Worth Department** woke a lot of people up all at once during an earlier broadcast this morning—with these words:

Jimmy Carter—roaring drunk and smashing up everything within reach—has been thrown out of the Moscow Olympics.

This is another Jimmy Carter. A Scottish member of the British swimming team.

That's not all.

In Detroit, a Jimmy Carter has been arrested for burglary . . .

And he was arrested by police officer Richard Nixon.

July 30, 1980

Our **For What It's Worth Department** knows there's a roadside sign on I-95 as you approach De Land, Florida.

The yellow diamond-shaped sign warns travelers: NARCOTICS INSPECTION AHEAD.

There is no inspection.

But drivers who see the sign panic and make an immediate illegal U-turn.

They are stopped and searched.

The American Civil Liberties Union is objecting.

May 10, 1989

Joe Griffith of Dallas informs our **For What It's Worth Department** . . .

Of the airline baggage handlers who retrieved an animal carrier in the luggage bay of an airliner . . .

But the dog in it was dead.

With visions of lawsuits dancing in their heads they advised the woman passenger that her dog had been mis-sent to another destination . . .

Promised they would find it.

They disposed of the dead dog.

Meanwhile they set out to search animal welfare agencies for a look-alike live dog.

They found one.

An airline baggage handler put the substitute dog in the animal carrier with the lady's name and address on it—delivered it to her front door.

She took one look and said, "That's not *my* dog!"

She said, "My dog is dead; I was bringing it home for burial."

April 30, 1987

Our **For What It's Worth Department** is told that Dennis Weidman is principal of Central School in Amboy, Illinois.

He made a wager with his school's fourth graders.

If they would read four books each in one month . . .

He pledged to climb a tree in the schoolyard and read another book to the youngsters—from up there in the tree.

They DID read four books each.

And Mr. Weidman DID climb the big elm tree.

He paused and stood on the first limb—but the youngsters below shouted, "Higher!"

He climbed higher.

They shouted, "Higher!"

And he laughed and climbed higher.

But then he stopped laughing and stopped climbing . . .

When one down below shouted, "Jump!"

May 11, 1989

69

Our **For What It's Worth Department** concludes that Orlando, Florida, has one prejudiced jury!

In the Orange County Courthouse . . .

A jury of twelve . . .

On their way to the courtroom . . .

The entire jury was stuck for twenty minutes in a courthouse elevator!

On their way to hear a case against Otis Elevator Company.

November 4, 1986

Our **For What It's Worth Department** visits Leeds, England, where Harold Fenby tried a hearing aid . . .

But his hearing continued to deteriorate.

He had the hospital fit this hearing aid . . .

But it didn't help.

So he resigned himself to deafness—for twenty years.

NOW he discovers—the hospital had installed the hearing aid in the wrong ear!

Switched over, he hears fine.

Twenty years!

Mr. Fenby says, quote, "Isn't that hilarious!"

End quote.

March 7, 1978

Our **For What It's Worth Department** hears from Oceanside, California.

Robber wearing a motorcycle helmet and carrying a gun strode into the branch bank . . .

Selected a teller who appeared fiftyish, soft, kindly, an easy mark . . .

And handed her a note demanding money or her life.

Money or I'll blow your head off—words to that effect.

The woman reached for the cash drawer . . .

Then she looked again at the note . . .

And her eyes flashed . . .

Her lips clenched . . .

She pulled the entire cash drawer out . . .

But instead of giving him money . . .

She clobbered the robber over the head with the drawer . . .

And again and again . . .

And she is scolding him . . .

Money is flying everywhere and she is beating him and shouting shame on him and bouncing blows off his helmet . . .

Until the young man turned and ran.

Police caught him in nearby shrubbery.

THEN they asked the woman teller . . .

How come she was about to give him money at gunpoint and then, suddenly, instead, became enraged?

She said, "In his note there was a very naughty word."

July 18, 1979

Our **For What It's Worth Department** is in Atlanta.

This traveling microphone is plugged in today in the handsome studios of WGST . . .

During the morning while I was preparing these notes . . .

A lady was interviewed by Dennis O'Hayre . . .

The lady is 103.

Eva Reitzel.

Would you like her formula for living to be a healthy, active 103?

Here it is in nine words:

Stay away from doctors—and stay away from men.

February 23, 1982

Our **For What It's Worth Department** reads *Grit:*

The Bartons of Sacramento were driving toward home in dark rain . . .

The parents in the front seat . . .

Their two little girls in the rear.

After a hundred miles of freeway they turned off on the last twenty miles of winding country road . . .

Suddenly to be confronted by another car's blinding headlights.

The other car was coming over the crest of a hill . . .

Mr. Barton saw the oncoming glare through his wet windshield, swerved off the road onto a muddy shoulder.

The car spun wildly in a circle, then fishtailed as Mr. Barton fought to regain control . . .

And finally, facing backward, stopped.

When Eloise Barton could catch her breath her first thought was the backseat; were the babies all right?

She turned to hear her five-year-old complain . . .

"I was asleep, Daddy. Do it again!"

March 15, 1984

F**or What It's Worth Department**—closed circuit for members of First Presbyterian Church, Columbia, California.

Your church board AUTHORIZED YOUR PASTOR'S ATTENDANCE at that week-long study conference . . .

A week-long retreat involving Bible study . . .

A STUDY conference.

It was a typographical misprint in your church bulletin which said Pastor Jim McCluskey will be away this week attending "a stud conference".

And yes it IS too late for others to sign up.

February 15, 1989

Our **For What It's Worth Department** understands B. J. Chandler is school superintendent in Dardanelle, Arkansas.

Reports the junior high girl came to school wearing one red sock and one blue sock.

When Mr. Chandler asked her the significance she said she was an "individualist".

She said, "I have a right to be different if I want to."

Then she added, "Besides, all the kids are doing it!"

December 1, 1981

Our **For What It's Worth Department** sympathizes with New Yorkers—whose resistance just gets worn down by the tribulations of Manhattan's everywhere and ever-present dangers.

Bob Herguth reports two women wearing mink coats entered a luxury apartment elevator in New York . . .

Before the doors closed a man got in leading a Doberman pinscher.

"Sit!" the man commanded.

And without a single word or a moment's wait the two women sat down right there on the elevator floor.

January 13, 1982

Our **For What It's Worth Department** is convinced John Robert Ford, 29, of Williamson, West Virginia —is a talker.

We'll see if he can talk himself out of this.

A Lexington, Kentucky, woman married him last March believing him to be football star Joe Montana.

And she became Mrs. Montana.

When this made news—another woman in Nashville recognized his picture.

Another wife.

She thought she had married Hank Williams's piano player.

She admits it was probably her fault that he left her.

She presented him with a San Francisco 49ers warm-up jacket.

That's when he decided to be Joe Montana.

August 20, 1986

Flint, Michigan, police tell our **For What It's Worth Department** they now have a computerized list of all unmarked police cars.

Flint, Michigan, police can now recognize one another—even in unmarked police cars—because they have this complete list.

It identifies makes, models, and license plate numbers of all unmarked police cars.

They got the list from local crooks during a drug raid.

March 9, 1989

Our **For What It's Worth Department** learns the Bible has been paraphrased AGAIN!

This time by a boy, age seven, in Soquel, California.

In Sunday School the children were encouraged to restate scripture in their own words.

The Schulz boy, age seven, chose the 23rd Psalm.

His version starts out: "The Lord is my shepherd; I don't want nuthin'".

November 8, 1984

Our **For What It's Worth Department** hears from Mary Meador of Kilgore, Texas.

Says she knows a local Kilgore executive who is back and forth to England so—he imported an English secretary.

Employed an English secretary and brought her here.

He, the executive, was on another business trip to England . . .

When his Texas office received a phone call.

And his secretary dutifully told the caller, "Oh, Mr. so-and-so—apparently you hadn't heard—Mr. Allen has gone to the United Kingdom."

The caller said, "I am sorry. Terribly sorry. Is it too late to send flowers?"

May 7, 1984

Q*uote* magazine offers our **For What It's Worth Department** . . .

The revelation . . .

The explanation . . .

For why football's John Madden is afraid of flying.

Madden confided it was something that happened years ago . . .

At an airport . . .

When he was standing in line at an insurance policy machine . . .

And noted that there were three pilots ahead of him.

October 2, 1986

Our **For What It's Worth Department** understands Dr. Roland Cross of Loyola Medical, Chicago—got a bill from the hospital.

The *doctor* got a bill.

$309 for anesthesia during Caesarean delivery.

Dr. Cross notified hospital auditors that he had not been hospitalized for any reason . . .

And certainly a seventy-year-old male would not be having a C-section.

The hospital blamed its computer.

But guess what?

Now Dr. Cross has been notified by Blue Cross that his hospital bill has been paid.

$309 for anesthesia—during Caesarean delivery—and Blue Cross further offers its congratulations on the birth of TWINS!

June 23, 1986

Our **For What It's Worth Department** sees that Harry Covert is contemplating running for state senate in Virginia.

Harry Covert, among other things, has been a Little League umpire.

He thought this would be an advantage.

But campaigning, he knocked on a door in Lynchburg . . .

To the woman who came to the door he said, "I'm Harry Covert."

She said, "I know who you are. You called my son out at home plate!"

And she slammed the door.

March 25, 1983

Our **For What It's Worth Department** intercepts a transmission near Orlando, Florida.

State trooper radios a truck jockey on his CB.

State trooper asks, "What is your speed?"

Truck driver replies, "Fifty-five, officer, just fifty-five."

State trooper radios back, "Then you'd better pull over and get out of the way—because I just clocked your trailer doing seventy!"

December 21, 1984

Our **For What It's Worth Department** reads *The Washingtonian* . . .

About the nine-year-old boy who announced to his parents that he had a date.

A date with a girl at the age of nine? His parents were taken aback.

But the lad had already telephoned the girl they'd met last summer and invited her to his house for dinner. He had lured her with the promise his mom would make popovers. And dad would get a VCR tape of *Thriller* at the video store.

So—the pretty little girl was delivered by her mother.

After dinner the two youngsters went down to the rec room and watched Michael Jackson.

At ten P.M. his father delivered them to her front door. Her four older sisters rushed out to hug and greet her. It was her first date also.

Back home, before the dying fire, dad sat soberly thinking about how fast babies grow up. His young son, misinterpreting his father's mood, walked over, put his hand on dad's shoulder and said, "Don't worry, Dad; nothing happened!"

May 8, 1984

For What It's Worth . . .

In a county jail in south Florida—jail officials found a plastic trash bag hanging to the bars of a cell.

Inside was Jimmy Jones.

A prisoner who hoped he'd get taken out with the trash.

And he might have . . .

Except during roll call his reflexes took over.

And when the name Jimmy Jones was called . . .

From inside the bag came a muffled response: "Here."

May 12, 1983

Our **For What It's Worth Department** concedes . . .

One to a customer.

In the church bulletin of St. Bernard's Church in Akron, Ohio, it says:

The church needs men to help serve during funerals during the week . . .

And nobody will have to serve EVERY week; the duty will be rotated.

And it says, *We do not have a large number of funerals at St. Bernard's; never more than one per person.*

End quote.

All right.

December 13, 1977

94

Alex Thein of the Milwaukee *Sentinel* tells our **For What It's Worth Department** . . .

Fred was a great practical joker.

When his three closest friends got married he played wedding night tricks on each.

Now Fred was getting married and he was quietly terrified of what THEY might do to HIM.

But nobody interrupted the minister.

Nobody sent naughty telegrams.

Nobody hid their suitcases or stole their champagne.

Not even a cake fight at the wedding reception.

When the honeymoon began Fred's car started readily. No flat tires. Nothing strange in the trunk. Not even any tin cans tied to the rear bumper.

Fred and his bride, relieved at their friends' restraint, left for their hotel.

THE NEXT MORNING . . .

Fred picked up the bedroom phone and dialed for room service and ordered breakfast for two.

From the CLOSET . . . came a voice:

"Hey, Fred, make that breakfast for FIVE. Okay?"

September 25, 1987

Our **For What It's Worth Department** hears from Jackson, Mississippi—where Lucille Goodyear reports all kinds of trouble driving to and from work.

She says it used to be easy . . .

No traffic problems . . .

No mad rat race . . .

But now, Wow! Cars coming from all directions.

She says it's been that way ever since she got her new glasses.

April 23, 1979

Our **For What It's Worth Department** found today's sue-er in Virginia Beach.

Eric Edmonds—determined to lose weight—went to Humana Hospital Bayside—and had his stomach stapled.

With staples surgeons shrank the size of his stomach.

But within forty-eight hours after the surgery he snuck out of his room and raided the hospital refrigerator and ate so much he burst his staples.

Mr. Edmonds is suing the hospital for a quarter million dollars for failure to keep its refrigerator locked.

June 10, 1987

For What It's Worth . . .

Entertainer Tom Jones had a photographer follow him into a public toilet on a British freeway.

The girl with the camera ran into the washroom and climbed over the door into his toilet cubicle . . .

He pushed her out the door.

Last words he heard her say were, "I'll never buy one of your records again!"

She did not say why.

May 24, 1982

Our **For What It's Worth Department** has an item of interest for Duncanville, Texas, suburban Dallas.

Your preschool PTA is holding a charity auction tomorrow.

Your *preschool* PTA is raising money.

You parents of preschoolers will be bidding on a prize donated by a local urologist . . .

A $500 vasectomy.

March 29, 1985

Our **For What It's Worth Department** wants to be sure you've noted this postscript to the Nevada primary election.

On the ballot voters voting for Democrat for state treasurer had quite a choice.

Any of five candidates.

List of five candidates or—there was a space marked "None of the above".

"None of the above" finished first!

September 4, 1986

Our **For What It's Worth Department** wonders if you heard about the customer who presented a credit card at David Burr—the Irving, Texas, clothing store.

Young woman presented this credit card to the cashier.

The cashier asked, "What is your name?"

Customer said, "Diane Klos."

Cashier asked, "And what is your address?"

Customer gave her address. It was the address on the credit card.

But the cashier announced, "You came to the wrong place. I am Diane Klos; that is my address and that is MY credit card."

And THEN she summoned police.

February 4, 1987

Our **For What It's Worth Department** says NOW it can be told:

Before the Carters left the White House . . .

Daughter Amy needed help with some homework.

It was a Friday and the homework assignment was due on Monday.

A question about the industrial revolution.

Neither she nor her mother quite understood the question, so mother Rosalyn asked a White House aide to ask the Labor Department.

Sunday afternoon a truck pulled up at the White House loaded with a computer printout.

Somebody assumed it was information the President urgently needed.

So the Labor Department had kept a full computer team working all weekend to prepare the information.

When mother Rosalyn was told that the research had cost hundreds of thousands of taxpayer dollars she was horrified.

But it was too late to do anything about it.

So the information was used to help Amy complete her homework.

On that homework assignment—Amy got a "C".

February 9, 1981

Larry Stone of Paducah, Kentucky, tells our **For What It's Worth Department** that he was recently on a plane from St. Louis preparing to land in Los Angeles.

He was in the washroom . . .

When he heard a rap on the door and a woman's voice said: "Don't forget to wash your hands, comb your hair and zip up your pants before you come out!"

Larry did as he was told.

Then came out to be greeted by a woman who suddenly turned beet red and almost fainted.

She said she'd thought her young son was in there.

Larry said he didn't mind being reminded.

October 18, 1990

Our **For What It's Worth Department** hears from Annelle Dugan, Kilgore, Texas . . .

About the local high school boy who had something of a reputation for . . .

Well, every girl in the school had experienced or heard of his approaches . . .

So his reputation had preceded him when this new girl in school dated him for the first time.

And sure enough—on a lonely road—he announced that his car had run out of gas.

And he moved closer.

And she removed from her handbag a gin bottle. Full of gasoline.

August 16, 1990

Our **For What It's Worth Department** has learned that Duane Cowgill, the barber in Marshall, Michigan, had such an abundant garden this year—he decided to share it.

Tomatoes, peppers, zucchini . . .

On a bench in front of his barbershop Duane placed a small mountain of his leftover produce, with a sign reading: FREE—HELP YOURSELF.

By the end of the day the produce was gone.

But Duane forgot to remove the sign.

And the next morning the bench was gone.

October 10, 1990

Our **For What It's Worth Department** understands it was Leon Cope's job to clear the snow off a big parking lot in Sun Valley.

It was a big job.

His pile of snow grew to twenty by forty feet.

He was dog tired.

When a passerby wanted to know now what was he going to do with all that snow . . .

Leon said he'd wait for it to dry out and then burn it.

February 12, 1982

Our **For What It's Worth Department** hears from Richmond, California—where Mrs. Lily Fowler, 80, drove into an automatic car wash yesterday.

Into and THROUGH!

Reaching for the brake, she hit the accelerator instead.

And the car sped ahead.

THROUGH the car wash . . .

Out into the busy street, where it struck another car . . .

And bounced into a parking lot fence and bounced off the fence . . .

And into a gas station gas pump . . .

Knocking the gas pump flat and spilling its gas on the ground.

Backing up, her car rammed another—and that set the spilled gasoline on fire.

And the fire burned both those cars plus two.

Passersby broke a window and got Mrs. Fowler out of her car—unhurt.

But embarrassed.

Her son is a city Fire Captain.

April 3, 1986

111

Mrs. Patricia Pitt of Ogden, Utah, tells our **For What It's Worth Department** that she presented her own small children . . .

With a videocassette . . .

And told them to have fun . . .

Which they did . . .

For forty minutes . . .

Watching what's called a "skin flick".

Forty minutes of steamy pornography.

Mrs. Pitt, horrified when she found out what it was, says she had not examined the cassette carefully when she'd rented it.

She'd noted only that the Disney cartoon character GOOFY was on the label.

She had not even read the title: *The Nine Ages of Nakedness.*

Her youngsters, all under age six, thought it was "funny".

August 9, 1984

For What It's Worth . . .

In the jailhouse in Boston a prisoner has chewed up and swallowed a razor blade . . .

But he refuses to allow himself to be X-rayed . . .

Says X-rays can be a hazard to your health!

January 30, 1980

Our **For What It's Worth Department** has learned that Duluth, Minnesota, is where a city councilman . . .

George Downs . . .

In City Hall . . .

Put his briefcase down while he put his coat on . . .

Put his briefcase down behind a statue in the lobby . . .

And forgot it . . .

Left it there . . .

When he went across the street for dinner.

He returned to City Hall in time to hear there'd been a "bomb threat".

But the bomb squad had taken care of it.

They had opened a mysterious briefcase—with a blast of high-pressure water—and the whole lobby was wallpapered with George's soggy, shredded papers.

April 16, 1986

Our **For What It's Worth Department** reads the Hudspeth County *Herald.*

Dell Valley motorist was stopped and ticketed for speeding.

The angry motorist said, "And just what am I supposed to do with this ticket?"

The officer had to be tempted.

But what he said was . . .

"Keep it."

He said, "When you get three you get a bicycle."

June 20, 1989

Our **For What It's Worth Department** hears that Speedy Morris—basketball coach for La Salle University—was shaving when his wife called out to tell him he was wanted on the phone by *Sports Illustrated.*

Speedy Morris was so excited by the prospect of national recognition that he nicked himself with his razor and ran—with a mixture of blood and lather on his face—and fell down the steps.

But he got to the phone.

And the voice on the other end said:

"For just seventy-five cents an issue you can get a one-year trial subscription . . ."

July 7, 1989

Our **For What It's Worth Department** returns to Tulsa, Oklahoma . . .

Where jurors were being questioned about their availability for a week-long trial in the courtroom of Judge Thomas Brett.

One prospective juror asked to be excused.

He said his wife was going to "conceive a baby".

Judge Brett asked, "Don't you mean she is going to *deliver* a baby?"

The man said, "No—she is going to conceive a baby."

Judge excused him from jury duty . . .

Said he was not sure he understood but, he said, "Either way you ought to be there."

March 26, 1981

Our **For What It's Worth Department** knows that when Grey Baker goes golfing in Jackson, Mississippi—he has taken his three-year-old grandson Trevor along as a companion . . .

The boy has been learning the game by watching.

Last week Grandpa Baker bought the lad a set of play golf clubs of his own.

This past weekend—during a family cookout in the backyard—the little lad who'd learned golf by observing Grandpa announced, "Watch me!"

And he said a no-no word and threw his golf club up into the pear tree.

November 3, 1986

Our **For What It's Worth Department** hears from a young mother, Vicki Marsh, who says she NOW knows the meaning of the phrase "generation gap" . . .

Says she borrowed a folk-song cassette from the library for her four-year-old daughter . . .

And now the little girl, believing she is imitating one of the songs on the tape, is singing loudly and proudly and repeatedly:

"Oh my darling, oh my darling, oh my darling . . . Calvin Klein!"

August 6, 1990

Our **For What It's Worth Department** wants to be sure you've heard about Jeannette Bruce . . .

She is a writer for *Sports Illustrated.*

Concerned about crime in New York, she took up judo—AND karate.

Both!

Learned all the kicks and pressure holds and punches—until she qualified as an expert in martial arts, plural!

So when a purse snatcher tried to snatch HER purse . . .

She hit him over the head with her umbrella.

September 14, 1990

Our **For What It's Worth Department** knows Vice President Dan Quayle is on the campaign trail—in Champaign-Urbana—campaigning for an Illinois politician, Representative Lynn Martin.

Organizers of the political rally got schoolchildren excused from school for the parade—asked the youngsters to wave and cheer when the motorcade came by.

And they did.

They did indeed wave and cheer.

Only trouble was that the first motorcade to come by was a FUNERAL!

September 24, 1990

Our **For What It's Worth Department** heard from Doc Blakely about a chap who traveled a lot . . .

And every time he was out of town his house was robbed.

The burglaries stopped after they arrested—his travel agent.

August 6, 1984

For What It's Worth . . .

Virginia Young—is cashier at McDonald's restaurant drive-up window in Des Peres, Missouri.

Cashier at the drive-up window.

She says enough of this customer.

He drives up to her window and orders a large Coke and he is wearing only a shirt.

Wearing nothing else. Just a shirt.

So she called police after he came in that way—regularly.

For a year.

June 20, 1986

Our **For What It's Worth Department** hears of a great escape!

Gary Tindle was in a California courtroom charged with robbery.

He asked and got from Judge Armando Rodriguez permission to go to the bathroom.

While the bathroom DOOR was guarded—Mr. Tindle climbed up onto the plumbing and opened a panel in the ceiling.

Sure enough, a dropped ceiling with space between.

He climbed up—and into the crawlspace—and headed south.

He'd gone thirty-some feet when the ceiling panels broke from under him and dropped him to the floor . . .

Right back in Judge Rodriguez's courtroom.

December 4, 1986

Our **For What It's Worth Department** reads Bo Whaley in the Dublin, Georgia, *Courier Herald* . . .

He reports a local third-grade geography assignment was for each pupil to stand and recite in a single sentence what he or she liked most about his or her home state of Georgia.

It was a third-grade girl who said, quote:

"I think we have the most beautiful state in the whole world; of course, I may be a little pregnant."

End quote.

August 12, 1986

Our **For What It's Worth Department** visits Raleigh, North Carolina, where a state cop stopped an obviously drunk driver.

While he was ticketing the man, there was a multicar accident on the other side of the divided highway.

The highway patrolman told the drunk to wait.

The patrolman went across the highway to sort out the accident.

After a while the drunk figured he'd waited long enough and he drove on home and told his wife that if anybody asked she should say he had been in bed with the flu all day.

Within the hour two state patrolmen appeared at the home of the drunk driver and asked to see him.

He came from the bedroom wrapped in a robe and coughing and wheezing.

The patrolmen asked if he had been driving that evening and he said he'd been sick in bed.

They apologized for bothering him and asked if they could take a look at his car.

The wrapped-up drunk escorted them to the garage and inside was—a highway patrol car, the blue lights still flashing.

January 15, 1986

Our **For What It's Worth Department** quotes *Quote* . . .

Young Wilbert Price rejoined mother in the shopping center carrying two ice-cream cones.

And announced they did not cost anything.

He explained that with an ice-cream cone in each hand he had asked the ice-cream saleslady to take the money out of his pants pocket.

But he admonished her to be careful—not to hurt his pet snake.

July 30, 1977

Our **For What It's Worth Department** appreciates the National Fire Academy in Emmitsburg, Maryland.

That's where good firemen go to become better firemen.

Thousands each year—career and volunteer firefighters—go to the National Fire Academy to learn the latest in fire prevention and fire fighting and fire department management.

On that campus the current class in fire prevention was challenged to compete . . .

Students at the National Fire Academy were sent forth to see which student could find the most fire code violations in any one building.

The winner of the competition found and confirmed the most—180 separate fire code violations in one building—WITHOUT LEAVING THE CAMPUS!

October 17, 1990

Our **For What It's Worth Department** wants you to meet the Gertsons of Gering, Nebraska.

Martha and Chris Gertson.

Every weekday afternoon at two . . .

Martha lowers the window shades . . .

Disconnects the phone . . .

And turns on TV . . .

To the wrestling matches.

Martha admits that she is a "Hulkamaniac" who loves to watch those big bruisers head-butt one another and body-slam one another—and when she gets sufficiently worked up she throws a stepover toe hold on her husband, Chris—and there on the floor in front of the TV set they try to pin each other.

Don't tell Martha Gertson that wrestling matches on TV are staged.

She says if there's anything on TV that's faked it's the soap operas.

She says the wrestling matches are for real.

Including hers with Chris.

Which she usually wins.

Martha Gertson is 76. Husband Chris is 82.

September 12, 1990

Our **For What It's Worth Department** has learned that in San Antonio, Texas, a priest has gone to court—to try to stop a member of his congregation from singing.

Father Alexander Wangler of Our Lady of Sorrows Church has tried every other way to get the woman to stop singing along with the church choir . . .

Now he is seeking a court order.

The problem is that she, in her pew, sings when the choir sings—but she sings only HER OWN COMPOSITIONS!

October 17, 1990

137

Our **For What It's Worth Department** doesn't know, but Tom Poole of Farmersville, Texas, swears it happened.

Two state policemen chased a speeder, caught up with him in Waxahachie.

The cop making out the ticket whispered to the other officer, "How do you spell Waxahachie?"

The second officer said he wasn't sure.

First officer said, "Let's let him go and catch up with him again down the road—in Waco."

January 6, 1989

The respected *American Medical News* confirms what our **For What It's Worth Department** is about to relay.

A patient complained of an earache. His right ear.

His doctor prescribed eardrops—an antibiotic.

Are you with me to here?

The doctor prescribed eardrops for an earache.

When the patient got the eardrops prescription filled the pharmacist wrote on the bottle . . .

Three drops in *r*—for *right*—ear.

No space and no punctuation.

For "right ear", the instructions on the bottle read: *r*—ear.

That spells *rear.*

The patient said later he knew it sounded like a strange remedy for an earache but he had dutifully applied the three drops to his rear for three days before the error was discovered.

January 15, 1982

Eddie Stephens, Palmetto, Georgia, writes our **For What It's Worth Department** . . .

About a local fledgling lawyer who was sitting in his new office waiting for his first client.

When he heard the outer door open he quickly tried to sound very busy.

As the man entered the office, the young lawyer is on the telephone saying, quote:

"Bill, I'm flying to New York on the Mitchell Brothers thing; it looks like it's going to be a biggie. Also we'll need to bring Carl in from Houston on the Cimarron case. By the way, Al Cunningham and Pete Finch want to come in with me as partners. Bill, you'll have to excuse me, somebody just came in. . . ."

He hung up.

Turned to the man who had just entered.

The young lawyer said, "Now, how can I help you?"

The man said, "I'm here to hook up the phone."

January 7, 1982

Our **For What It's Worth Department** understands Bob's Famous Ice Cream Parlor in Bethesda, Maryland, was robbed but . . .

Manager Nathan Peabody was warned in time.

By telephone:

"You are the manager? Listen carefully. This is the police. You are going to be robbed. Do NOT resist. Let the robber have your money. Our police will be waiting for him right outside your store and we need to catch him with the money on him. Thank you for your cooperation."

Mr. Peabody cooperated.

Man with scruffy beard and a knife came in, demanded money.

Mr. Peabody emptied the cash register and gave it to him.

The bearded man with the knife took the money and left the store and kept going and kept going . . .

Then Mr. Peabody called police and said, "I have been had!"

March 26, 1986

Our **For What It's Worth Department** has learned that Mrs. Gladys Gibbons is suing the man who was teaching her to drive a car.

Mrs. Gladys Gibbons of London is suing her driving instructor.

She tells High Court that it was all his fault.

That during her nineteenth driving lesson . . .

Let me quote her precisely from the transcript of yesterday's court proceedings.

Mrs. Gladys Gibbons, 55, says, quote:

"If he"—meaning Howard Priestly, the driving instructor—

"If he had just reached over and hit the brake or switched off the ignition—I might never have hit that tree. But no—all he did was to brace himself, close his eyes, and shout: 'Now you've bloody done it!' "

End quote.

She charges "negligence", wants him to pay the damages.

February 28, 1978

*G*rit tells our **For What It's Worth Depart-**
ment . . .

A woman from Lansing, Michigan, was vacation-
ing in Florida . . .

Found a secluded spot on the roof of the hotel for
sunbathing . . .

Took off her clothing to get tan all over.

Within half an hour the hotel manager was beside
her insisting that she cover up.

No, he agreed, nobody was in sight . . .

But she was stretched out on the dining room
skylight!

February 15, 1980

For What It's Worth . . .

In Sandpoint, Idaho, a pilot named Kurt Johnson was arrested . . .

The plane he flew from Spokane . . .

The Cessna 150 in which he arrived Sandpoint . . .

Had been stolen in Spokane.

That's what the Sandpoint police say. That he stole the plane.

But Mr. Johnson says that is NOT the way it happened at all.

Mr. Johnson says . . .

That he was "sucked into town through a black hole".

And he says that "Captain Kirk of the starship *Enterprise*" is coming to rescue him at any moment.

March 23, 1983

146

The Sullivan, Missouri, *Independent News* informs our **For What It's Worth Department** . . .

Four high school boys skipped morning classes . . .

Arrived late to tell the teacher the car they shared had a flat tire.

She smiled sympathetically. But the teacher explained they'd missed a test that morning.

So she told the boys to take seats apart from one another, get out paper and pencil and answer this question:

"Which tire was flat?"

September 24, 1986

Our **For What It's Worth Department** couldn't resist . . .

Traveling executive Tom Haggai telephoned his wife from an airport pay telephone, concluded the call, said good-bye and replaced the receiver.

As he was walking away the phone rang.

Oh-oh . . .

Probably the operator telling him he'd talked more than he'd paid for.

It was the operator.

But instead of asking for more coins she said, quote:

"Sir, I thought you'd like to know—just after you hung up—your wife said she loves you."

May 18, 1983

149